Contents

1   Chapter 1: Understanding Bitcoin and Halving...2

　1.1   Introduction to Bitcoin...2

　1.2   The Role of Halving..4

　1.3   Historical Performance...5

2   Chapter 2: Preparing for Halving 2024...7

　2.1   Market Analysis...7

　2.2   Investor Sentiment...9

　2.3   Risk Management...11

3   Chapter 3: The Halving Event..13

　3.1   The Halving Process..13

　3.2   Price Volatility..15

　3.3   Market Reaction...17

4   Chapter 4: Post-Halving Investment Strategies..19

　4.1   Long-Term Investment...19

　4.2   Trading Opportunities..21

　4.3   Diversification..23

5   Chapter 5: Technical Analysis and Indicators...25

　5.1   Technical Analysis...25

　5.2   Chart Patterns...27

　5.3   Fundamental Analysis...29

6   Chapter 6: Navigating Regulatory Challenges..31

　6.1   Regulatory Landscape...31

　6.2   Compliance and Security...33

　6.3   Institutional Adoption...35

7   Chapter 7: Future Outlook and Beyond...37

　7.1   Industry Trends:...37

　7.2   Bitcoin's Role:..39

　7.3   Investor Mindset..41

8   Conclusion:..42

Introduction:

Welcome to "Bitcoin Halving 2024: A Guide for Investors." In this book, we will explore the concept of Bitcoin halving and its potential impact on the cryptocurrency market. We will delve into the significance of the upcoming halving event in 2024 and provide valuable insights on what investors should consider after the halving to make informed decisions. Whether you are a seasoned investor or new to the world of Bitcoin, this book aims to equip you with the knowledge necessary to navigate the post-halving landscape successfully.

1 Chapter 1: Understanding Bitcoin and Halving

1.1 Introduction to Bitcoin

A brief overview of Bitcoin and its emergence as a decentralized digital currency.

In 2009, the world witnessed the birth of a groundbreaking concept: Bitcoin, the first decentralized digital currency. Emerging amidst the global financial crisis, Bitcoin promised a radical departure from traditional, centralized financial systems. This revolutionary technology, shrouded in the mystery of its anonymous creator Satoshi Nakamoto, has since captured the imagination of investors, technologists, and even governments. Let's delve into the story of Bitcoin's emergence and explore its impact on the financial landscape.

From Whitepaper to Reality:

Bitcoin's journey began in 2008 with the publication of a whitepaper that outlined a peer-to-peer electronic cash system. This paper introduced the concept of blockchain, a distributed ledger technology that serves as the backbone of Bitcoin. Unlike traditional currencies controlled by central authorities, Bitcoin operates on a decentralized network. Transactions are verified and recorded by participants (miners) in the network, eliminating the need for intermediaries.

Key Features of a Decentralized System:

Transparency: All transactions are publicly viewable on the blockchain, creating an immutable record of financial activity.

Security: Cryptography secures transactions, making them resistant to tampering or fraud.

Censorship-resistance: No single entity controls the network, making it difficult to block or censor transactions.

Pseudo-anonymity: While transactions are traceable, user identities remain pseudonymous.

Impact and Challenges: Since its inception, Bitcoin has experienced a rollercoaster ride, marked by periods of explosive growth and dramatic crashes. Despite its volatility, it has sparked widespread interest in cryptocurrencies and blockchain technology. Here are some key impacts:

Financial Inclusion: Bitcoin offers access to financial services for individuals excluded from traditional banking systems.

Cross-border payments: International transactions can be faster and cheaper with Bitcoin compared to traditional methods.

Innovation: Blockchain technology has the potential to revolutionize various industries beyond finance.

Regulation: Governments are still grappling with how to regulate cryptocurrencies, leading to uncertainty for investors and businesses.

Scalability: The current Bitcoin network faces limitations in processing transactions, hindering widespread adoption.

Environmental concerns: The energy-intensive mining process raises concerns about sustainability.

Looking Ahead:

Bitcoin's story is far from over. As the technology evolves and regulations emerge, its future impact on financial systems remains uncertain. However, one thing is clear: Bitcoin's emergence has ignited a revolution in decentralized finance, and its disruptive potential continues to unfold.

Explaining the concept of halving and its significance in the Bitcoin network.

Imagine a revolutionary technology designed to have a finite supply, like a futuristic treasure chest with a limited number of gold coins. This is the core concept behind Bitcoin, and the "halving" mechanism plays a crucial role in maintaining its scarcity and potential value.

What is Halving?

A Bitcoin halving is a pre-programmed event that occurs approximately every four years, where the reward for mining new blocks gets cut in half. Initially, miners received 50 BTC per block, then it went down to 25, then 12.5, and currently sits at 6.25 BTC per block. The next halving, expected in April 2024, will further reduce this reward to 3.125 BTC.

Significance of Halving:

This seemingly simple reduction has profound implications for the Bitcoin network

Scarcity:

By limiting the rate at which new Bitcoins are created, halving mimics the finite nature of precious metals like gold, potentially making each remaining Bitcoin more valuable over time.

Mining Incentive:

While the block reward reduces, transaction fees for miners become increasingly important. This incentivizes miners to prioritize verifying transactions over simply acquiring new Bitcoins.

Network Security:

As mining becomes less profitable due to reduced rewards, only miners with efficient hardware and access to cheap electricity can remain competitive. This helps maintain the security of the network.

Price Impact:

Historically, Bitcoin price has experienced significant increases following halving events. However, this correlation isn't guaranteed, and other factors like market sentiment and regulations also play a role.

Beyond the Hype:

It's important to remember that halving is just one aspect of Bitcoin's complex ecosystem. Factors like adoption, regulation, and technological advancements will also influence its future. While potential for increased value exists, investing in Bitcoin carries inherent risks as with any volatile asset.

Impact on mining difficulty: Research how decreasing rewards affect the difficulty of mining new blocks.

Historical price trends: Analyze how past halving events have impacted Bitcoin's price.

Alternative theories: Explore different perspectives on the long-term impact of halving.

Regulation and its role: Understand how government regulations might affect Bitcoin's future.

By understanding the concept of halving and its significance, you gain valuable insight into the inner workings of this innovative technology and its potential impact on the financial landscape.

1.3 Historical Performance

An examination of the previous halving events and their impact on Bitcoin's price and market dynamics.

The Bitcoin halving, an event programmed to occur every 210,000 blocks (roughly every four years), is a crucial feature of the network. By cutting the block reward for miners in half, it reduces the rate at which new Bitcoins enter circulation, mimicking a finite resource like gold. But how has this halving actually impacted Bitcoin's price and market dynamics? Let's examine previous halving events and their results:

The First Halving (November 2012):

Pre-halving: Price hovered around $12.

Post-halving: Price rose steadily, reaching $200 within a year.

The Second Halving (July 2016):

Pre-halving: Price fluctuated between $300-$400.

Post-halving: Price experienced a correction, then slowly climbed, surpassing $19,000 by December 2017.

The Third Halving (May 2020):

Pre-halving: Price hovered around $8,000.

Post-halving: Price surged dramatically, reaching a peak of nearly $69,000 in November 2021.

Price increases: While not immediate, all three halvings were followed by significant price increases, ranging from 16X to nearly 850X.

Delayed impact: The price hikes didn't happen immediately after the halving, suggesting other factors also influenced the market.

Market sentiment: Anticipation surrounding the halving often plays a role in driving up prices before the event.

Correlation, not causation: It's crucial to remember that correlation doesn't equal causation. Other factors like institutional adoption, regulation, and major global events can also impact price movements.

Scarcity: Reduced supply due to halving creates artificial scarcity, potentially driving up demand and price.

Mining profitability: With lower rewards, miners must become more efficient, impacting network security and hash rate.

Institutional investment: Growing interest from institutional investors can significantly influence price movements.

Regulation:

Regulatory decisions surrounding cryptocurrencies can create uncertainty and affect market sentiment.

Looking Ahead:

The next halving is expected in April 2024. While past trends suggest potential price increases, it's crucial to avoid making predictions based solely on historical data. Understanding the interplay of various factors, including market sentiment, regulations, and technological advancements, is vital for informed analysis.

Further Exploration:

Analyze price charts and technical indicators before and after each halving.

Research various theories on the long-term impact of halving on Bitcoin's price.

Explore studies on the relationship between market sentiment and Bitcoin price movements.

Discuss the potential impact of upcoming regulations on Bitcoin's future.

By examining past halving events and their impact, we gain valuable insights into Bitcoin's intricate relationship with supply, demand, and market dynamics. However, it's important to approach future predictions with caution and consider the multitude of factors that can influence this ever-evolving market.

2 Chapter 2: Preparing for Halving 2024

2.1 Market Analysis

Evaluating the state of the cryptocurrency market leading up to the halving event.

As the highly anticipated Bitcoin halving looms in April 2024, the cryptocurrency market finds itself in a state of flux. Evaluating its current state is crucial for anyone navigating this volatile landscape, considering both potential opportunities and lurking pitfalls.

Fear and Greed Index: Is the market dominated by fear or euphoria? This can dictate buying and selling behaviors, impacting prices.

Media Coverage: Is positive or negative press dominating the headlines? Public perception can significantly influence market trends.

Regulatory landscape: Are there impending regulations that could create uncertainty or instill confidence? Regulatory clarity can significantly affect market stability.

Price charts and indicators: Are technical indicators suggesting bullish or bearish patterns? Analyzing historical data can provide insights into potential future movements.

On-chain analysis: Are on-chain metrics like transaction volume and active addresses signaling increasing or decreasing user engagement? These metrics can reveal underlying market activity.

Alternative coin correlations: How are other major cryptocurrencies performing? Assessing correlations can help build a broader market picture.

Adoption and use cases: Are there new developments driving real-world use of cryptocurrencies? Increased adoption signals potential long-term value.

Institutional investment: Are major institutions entering the crypto space? Institutional involvement can bring stability and legitimacy.

Technological advancements: Are there significant innovations within the blockchain space? Technological advancements can unlock new possibilities and boost investor confidence.

Pre-Halving Hype vs. Reality: Past halving events have been followed by significant price increases, fueling the "halving hype" narrative. However, it's crucial to remember:

Correlation is not causation: Previous price surges might not be directly attributable to the halving itself.

Market sentiment plays a major role: Anticipation and speculation can create temporary bubbles that may not reflect long-term value.

External factors are at play: Global events, economic conditions, and regulatory decisions can significantly impact the market.

The Takeaway: Instead of solely focusing on the "halving hype," a prudent approach involves comprehensive analysis. Consider market sentiment, technical indicators, fundamental factors, and external influences. Remember, the crypto market is inherently volatile, and any predictions should be made with caution and a healthy dose of skepticism.

For further exploration:

Compare historical price movements before and after previous halving events.

Research expert opinions and predictions regarding the upcoming halving.

Analyze fundamental developments within specific projects you're interested in.

Stay informed about regulatory updates and their potential impact on the market.

By adopting a comprehensive and informed approach, you can navigate the pre-halving period with greater clarity and make sound decisions in this dynamic and ever-evolving market. Remember, there are no guarantees in the crypto space, and responsible investing requires careful consideration of both potential rewards and risks.

Analyzing the sentiment and expectations of investors before the halving.

With the Bitcoin halving event fast approaching in April 2024, a palpable buzz hangs over the cryptocurrency market. Understanding the sentiment and expectations of investors becomes crucial in navigating this period of heightened anticipation and potential volatility. Let's dive into the minds of investors and analyze their hopes, fears, and predictions:

1. Bullish Optimism:

Historical precedent: Many investors point to past halving events, specifically the dramatic price surges that followed. This fuels optimism, with hopes for a similar repeat performance.

Scarcity narrative: The impending reduction in new Bitcoin supply reinforces the "digital gold" narrative, leading some to believe in increased scarcity and rising value.

Institutional adoption: Growing involvement from institutional investors like hedge funds and corporations instills confidence in the long-term potential of Bitcoin.

2. Cautious Skepticism:

Overheated market: Some investors fear the market is already overvalued, and the halving might not trigger the expected price increase.

Regulation overhang: Regulatory uncertainty, particularly from major economies, creates apprehension and can dampen bullish enthusiasm.

Past performance: Not all halving events resulted in immediate price surges, reminding investors of potential deviations from historical patterns.

3. Fearful Uncertainty:

Volatility concerns: The inherent volatility of the crypto market worries some investors, who fear the halving could exacerbate price swings.

External factors: Global economic events, geopolitical tensions, and other external factors can create anxiety and influence investment decisions.

FOMO vs. FUD: The fear of missing out (FOMO) battles against the fear, uncertainty, and doubt (FUD) surrounding the event, creating emotional conflict for investors.

Expectations Management: It's crucial to approach any predictions surrounding the halving with a healthy dose of skepticism. While historical patterns and technical indicators offer valuable insights, numerous factors beyond the halving itself can impact the market.

Focus on fundamentals: Invest based on the long-term potential of projects, not solely on speculative hype surrounding the halving.

Diversify your portfolio: Spread your investments across various assets to mitigate risk and exposure to market volatility.

Manage your emotions: Stay informed but avoid making impulsive decisions driven by fear or euphoria.

Moving Forward:

The upcoming halving presents both opportunities and challenges for investors. By understanding the sentiment and expectations, coupled with responsible investment practices, individuals can navigate this period with greater awareness and make informed decisions aligned with their risk tolerance and financial goals.

Further Exploration:

Analyze investor surveys and sentiment gauges to gain insights into market psychology.

Research analyst reports and predictions from various sources to broaden your perspective.

Explore historical data and technical indicators to identify potential price patterns.

Stay updated on regulatory developments and their potential impact on the market.

Remember, informed and responsible investing, coupled with emotional detachment, is key to navigating the dynamic and often unpredictable world of cryptocurrency markets, especially during major events like the halving.

Strategies and techniques for managing risk during periods of market uncertainty.

Navigating the financial world is rarely smooth sailing, and periods of uncertainty can be particularly treacherous. Whether it's a looming recession, geopolitical tensions, or simply unexpected market fluctuations, these times call for a proactive approach to manage risk and protect your investments. Here are some key strategies and techniques to consider:

1. Revisit Your Risk Tolerance:

Self-assessment: Honestly assess your comfort level with potential losses. Remember, risk tolerance is unique and can evolve over time.

Adjust asset allocation: Align your portfolio composition with your risk profile. Consider reducing exposure to volatile assets and increasing holdings in safer options like bonds or cash equivalents.

2. Diversify, Diversify, Diversify:

Spread the risk: Invest across different asset classes (stocks, bonds, real estate, etc.) and within each class (diversify by sector, geography, etc.). This mitigates the impact of losses in any one area.

Explore non-correlated assets: Seek options that don't move in sync with the broader market, like gold or alternative investments.

3. Embrace Prudent Risk Management Techniques:

Stop-loss orders: Set pre-determined points where you automatically sell an asset to limit potential losses.

Hedging strategies: Use financial instruments like options or futures to offset potential losses in other holdings.

Dollar-cost averaging: Invest fixed amounts at regular intervals to average out the cost per share and reduce the impact of market volatility.

4. Stay Informed and Adapt:

Closely monitor market developments: Keep yourself updated on economic data, news, and potential risks on the horizon.

Rebalance your portfolio regularly: Adjust your asset allocation as market conditions and your risk tolerance evolve.

Stay calm and avoid emotional decisions: Fear and greed can cloud judgment. Stick to your investment plan and avoid knee-jerk reactions.

5. Consider Seeking Professional Guidance:

Financial advisors: A qualified advisor can personalize your risk management strategy based on your specific goals and risk tolerance.

Investment managers: For complex portfolios, consider professional management to navigate volatile markets effectively.

Remember:

There's no single "silver bullet" for risk management. Combine these strategies to create a customized approach that suits your needs.

Risk management is an ongoing process, not a one-time event. Continuously monitor, adjust, and adapt your strategies based on changing market conditions.

While minimizing risk is essential, seeking returns shouldn't be entirely abandoned. Remember the potential for positive outcomes even in uncertain times.

By incorporating these strategies and maintaining a proactive approach, you can navigate market uncertainty with greater confidence and protect your investments for the long haul.

3 Chapter 3: The Halving Event

3.1 The Halving Process

A detailed explanation of how the halving event unfolds and its effects on the Bitcoin supply.

The Bitcoin halving, occurring approximately every four years, is a critical event that directly impacts the supply of new Bitcoins and potentially influences its value. Let's delve into the mechanics of this event and its effects on the overall Bitcoin supply:

1. The Mechanism:

Block Reward: Every time a new block of transactions is verified and added to the blockchain, miners receive a block reward - currently 6.25 BTC.

Halving Code: Bitcoin's code is programmed to automatically reduce the block reward in half every 210,000 blocks, which roughly translates to every four years.

Impact on Miners: With a lowered reward, mining becomes less profitable, potentially leading to:

Increased competition: Only miners with efficient hardware and access to cheap electricity can remain competitive.

Network security: As less profitable miners drop off, the remaining miners become more important for network security.

Transaction fees: As block rewards decrease, transaction fees play a larger role in incentivizing miners.

2. Effects on Bitcoin Supply:

Scarcity: The primary goal of halving is to gradually reduce the rate at which new Bitcoins are created, mimicking a finite resource like gold.

Total Supply Cap: Bitcoin has a predefined maximum supply of 21 million coins. With each halving, the remaining number of coins to be mined gets smaller, ultimately reaching the limit around the year 2140.

Supply Dynamics: The halving reduces the **rate** of new coin creation, not the total number already mined. However, it impacts the distribution of new coins over time, front-loading the supply in the early years and slowing it down significantly later.

3. Potential Consequences:

Price fluctuations: Historically, halving events have been followed by significant price increases for Bitcoin. However, this correlation doesn't guarantee future outcomes, and other factors like market sentiment and regulations play a role.

Increased mining difficulty: As less profitable miners leave, the remaining miners compete for fewer rewards, leading to increased difficulty in solving the cryptographic puzzles and verifying blocks.

Sustainability concerns: Bitcoin mining requires significant energy consumption. As it becomes less profitable, miners might resort to less efficient methods, raising sustainability concerns.

Beyond the Hype:

It's crucial to remember that the halving is just one aspect of Bitcoin's complex ecosystem. While it can influence supply and potentially value, numerous other factors like adoption, regulation, and technological advancements will determine its long-term trajectory.

For further exploration:

Analyze historical price movements before and after previous halving events.

Research different theories on the long-term impact of halving on Bitcoin's price and supply.

Explore alternative cryptocurrencies with different supply dynamics and compare their characteristics.

Discuss the potential for alternative mining methods that could address sustainability concerns.

By understanding the technical details and potential implications of the halving event, you gain valuable insights into the inner workings of this innovative technology and its potential impacts on the financial landscape.

Understanding the potential short-term price volatility associated with the halving and how to navigate it.

As the Bitcoin halving event rapidly approaches on April 2024, anticipation and uncertainty fill the air. While the potential for long-term value appreciation exists, the event is likely to trigger short-term price volatility, creating challenges and opportunities for investors. Let's explore the potential causes of volatility and strategies to navigate it effectively.

1. Potential Causes of Price Volatility:

Increased Speculation: The hype surrounding the halving can attract speculative investors, leading to rapid price swings based on sentiment rather than fundamentals.

Short-Term Supply Shock: The immediate reduction in new Bitcoin supply might initially outpace demand, causing temporary price fluctuations.

Market Manipulation: High volatility attracts opportunists who may attempt to manipulate prices through techniques like coordinated buying/selling or spreading misinformation.

External Factors: Global economic events, geopolitical tensions, and regulatory changes can significantly impact the broader market, amplifying volatility in Bitcoin.

2. Strategies for Navigating Volatility:

Understand your risk tolerance: Be honest about your comfort level with potential losses and adjust your investment strategy accordingly.

Stick to your investment plan: Avoid impulsive decisions driven by fear or greed. Stay focused on your long-term goals and resist FOMO (fear of missing out).

Diversify your portfolio: Spread your risk across different asset classes, including less volatile options, to mitigate exposure to Bitcoin's price swings.

Dollar-cost averaging: Invest fixed amounts at regular intervals to average out the cost per Bitcoin and reduce the impact of volatility.

Utilize stop-loss orders: Set pre-determined prices at which your Bitcoin automatically sells, limiting potential losses if the price drops sharply.

Stay informed but manage emotions: Closely monitor the market but avoid letting news and social media hype influence your decisions.

Consider seeking professional guidance: For complex portfolios or high-risk tolerance, consulting a financial advisor can help create a personalized strategy.

Remember:

Predicting short-term price movements is notoriously difficult. While the halving may lead to volatility, it doesn't guarantee a specific direction or magnitude.

Volatility can present opportunities for experienced traders, but it also carries significant risks. Only invest what you can afford to lose.

Focus on the long-term potential of Bitcoin based on its underlying technology, adoption, and utility, not solely on short-term price movements.

By understanding the potential causes of volatility and employing sound investment strategies, you can navigate the halving period with greater confidence and protect your capital while remaining open to potential long-term gains.

Examining historical patterns and market reactions after previous halving events.

With the Bitcoin halving event fast approaching in April 2024, historical precedent becomes a powerful tool for analysis. By examining past halving events and the market's reactions, we can gain valuable insights into potential future scenarios, understand recurring patterns, and navigate the inherent volatility with greater awareness.

1. Diving into the Data:

Past Halvings: Three halving events have occurred since Bitcoin's inception:

November 2012 (block reward reduced from 50 BTC to 25 BTC)

July 2016 (reward reduced from 25 BTC to 12.5 BTC)

May 2020 (reward reduced from 12.5 BTC to 6.25 BTC)

Market Reactions: Following each halving, Bitcoin experienced significant price increases:

2012: Price rose from around $12 to $200 within a year.

2016: Price corrected initially but climbed to over $19,000 by December 2017.

2020: Price surged dramatically, reaching a peak of nearly $69,000 in November 2021.

2. Key Observations:

Price increases weren't immediate: While a general upward trend emerged after each halving, it wasn't always an immediate jump. Timeframes and magnitudes varied.

Other factors played a role: Market sentiment, institutional adoption, and external events also significantly influenced price movements.

Correlation not causation: Historical trends don't guarantee future outcomes. Each halving occurs within a different market context, making predictions challenging.

Looking Beyond the Numbers: While historical data offers valuable insights, it's crucial to consider additional factors when analyzing potential future outcomes:

Evolving market landscape: Increased institutional involvement, regulatory developments, and advancements in blockchain technology can significantly impact market dynamics.

Investor expectations: The anticipation surrounding the halving can fuel speculation and potentially exaggerate the price movements.

Psychological factors: Fear of missing out (FOMO) and fear, uncertainty, and doubt (FUD) can influence investor behavior and create volatility.

Navigating the Upcoming Halving: Instead of solely relying on historical patterns, consider a comprehensive approach.

Technical analysis: Utilize technical indicators and chart patterns to identify potential support and resistance levels.

Fundamental analysis: Assess Bitcoin's long-term value based on its underlying technology, adoption, and future potential.

Market sentiment analysis: Stay informed about investor sentiment and news flow to gauge overall market confidence.

Risk management: Diversify your portfolio and set stop-loss orders to mitigate potential losses.

Remember:

The crypto market is inherently volatile, and past performance is not a guarantee of future results. Utilize historical data as a reference point, but base your investment decisions on a thorough understanding of current market conditions, your risk tolerance, and your long-term investment goals.

By approaching the halving with a well-rounded perspective and responsible investment practices, you can navigate this dynamic period with greater clarity and make informed decisions aligned with your financial objectives.

4 Chapter 4: Post-Halving Investment Strategies

4.1 Long-Term Investment

Assessing the benefits and risks of holding Bitcoin as a long-term investment.

Investing in Bitcoin, the first and most popular cryptocurrency, promises both exciting potential and daunting risks. Before diving in, it's crucial to weigh the benefits and drawbacks of holding Bitcoin as a long-term investment:

1. Benefits:

High Growth Potential: Bitcoin's historical price performance has been remarkable, offering significant returns for early investors. Its finite supply and increasing demand could fuel further growth in the future.

Digital Gold Narrative: Some view Bitcoin as "digital gold," a hedge against inflation and a store of value in a digital age. Its scarcity and decentralized nature appeal to investors seeking an alternative to traditional assets.

Technological Innovation: The underlying blockchain technology has the potential to revolutionize various industries, potentially increasing Bitcoin's long-term value as its adoption expands.

Accessibility and Liquidity: Bitcoin can be bought and sold 24/7 from anywhere in the world, offering access to a global market with high liquidity.

2. Risks:

Extreme Volatility: Bitcoin's price can experience dramatic swings, leading to significant losses. This volatility can be stressful for investors and make it difficult to predict future returns.

Regulatory Uncertainty: Governments are still grappling with regulating cryptocurrencies, which can create uncertainty and potentially impact market stability.

Security Concerns: Hacks and scams targeting crypto exchanges and wallets pose a risk to Bitcoin holders. Secure storage and responsible handling are crucial.

Limited Use Cases: Currently, Bitcoin mainly functions as an investment asset. Its widespread adoption as a means of payment is still limited, impacting its real-world utility.

Environmental Impact: Bitcoin mining requires significant energy consumption, raising concerns about its sustainability and potential environmental damage.

Making an Informed Decision: Investing in Bitcoin requires careful consideration. Here are some key takeaways:

Don't invest more than you can afford to lose: The high volatility makes it a risky investment. Only invest what you're comfortable potentially losing completely.

Diversify your portfolio: Don't put all your eggs in one basket. Spread your investments across different asset classes to mitigate risk.

Do your own research: Understand the technology, the market, and the risks involved before investing. Don't rely solely on hype or speculation.

Focus on long-term potential: While short-term price fluctuations can be tempting, focus on Bitcoin's long-term potential and its place in the evolving financial landscape.

Stay informed: Keep up-to-date with developments in the cryptocurrency market, regulations, and the broader economic climate.

Remember:

Bitcoin is a complex and dynamic asset. There's no guarantee of success, and its future remains uncertain. By understanding the potential benefits and risks, conducting thorough research, and following a responsible investment strategy, you can make an informed decision about whether Bitcoin aligns with your long-term investment goals and risk tolerance.

Exploring potential trading opportunities that may arise following the halving.

The upcoming Bitcoin halving in April 2024 has traders and investors buzzing with anticipation. While predicting the future is impossible, analyzing potential trading opportunities can equip you to react swiftly and capitalize on market movements. Remember, **volatility is to be expected**, and responsible risk management is paramount.

Potential Scenarios:

1. Bullish Breakout:

Price Surge: Following historical trends, the halving could trigger a significant price increase due to reduced supply and increased demand.

Technical Analysis: Watch for bullish chart patterns and technical indicators suggesting upward momentum.

Long Positions: Consider entering long positions after a confirmed breakout above key resistance levels.

Profit Taking: Plan your exit strategy beforehand to lock in profits and manage risk.

2. Short-Term Correction:

Profit Taking: Some investors might sell after the initial hype, leading to a temporary price dip.

Technical Analysis: Monitor support levels and identify potential oversold conditions.

Short-Term Trades: Short-term traders could seek to profit from the correction by entering short positions.

Caution: Be aware of the potential for a reversal and have clear stop-loss orders in place.

3. Extended Volatility:

Increased Speculation: The hype surrounding the halving could amplify already high volatility.

Technical Analysis: Focus on price action and identify key support and resistance levels.

Scalping Strategies: Experienced traders might employ scalping strategies to profit from small price movements.

Risk Management: Strict risk management is crucial due to the unpredictable nature of volatile markets.

4. Emerging Opportunities:

Alternative Coins: Explore other cryptocurrencies potentially impacted by the halving narrative.

Derivatives: Utilize options contracts to hedge your positions or speculate on price movements.

Decentralized Finance (DeFi): Look for potential trading opportunities within the DeFi ecosystem.

5. Key Reminders:

Do your own research: Don't base your decisions solely on speculation or hype. Understand the market, the risks involved, and your own risk tolerance.

Manage your emotions: Stay calm and avoid impulsive decisions driven by fear or greed.

Have a plan: Develop a trading strategy based on your analysis and risk tolerance, including entry and exit points.

Diversify your portfolio: Don't put all your eggs in one basket. Spread your investments across different assets to mitigate risk.

Remember:

The halving is just one factor impacting the crypto market. Always consider the broader economic landscape, regulations, and investor sentiment. While potential opportunities exist, responsible trading practices and risk management are essential for navigating the post-halving landscape successfully.

4.3 Diversification

Discussing the importance of diversifying one's investment portfolio beyond Bitcoin.

Bitcoin, the pioneer of cryptocurrencies, has captured the imagination of investors worldwide. However, while its potential for growth is undeniable, it's crucial to remember diversification is key to a healthy and resilient investment portfolio. Here's why venturing beyond Bitcoin is critical:

1. Mitigating Risk:

Volatility: Bitcoin is renowned for its dramatic price swings, making it a high-risk asset. Diversifying helps spread risk across different assets, potentially minimizing losses if Bitcoin experiences a downturn.

Uncertain Future: Despite its popularity, Bitcoin's future remains uncertain. Regulatory changes, technological advancements, and unforeseen events could impact its value significantly. Diversification protects against unforeseen risks specific to Bitcoin.

2. Maximizing Potential:

Exposure to Different Opportunities: The cryptocurrency landscape extends far beyond Bitcoin. Diversifying allows you to tap into the potential of other promising projects with unique functionalities and use cases, potentially boosting your overall returns.

Hedging Against Correlation: Cryptocurrencies exhibit varying degrees of correlation with Bitcoin. Diversifying with less correlated assets can help smooth out portfolio returns and reduce overall volatility.

3. Aligning with Investment Goals:

Different Risk Profiles: Not all investors have the same risk tolerance. Diversification allows you to choose assets that align with your individual risk appetite, ensuring comfortable and sustainable investment practices.

Diversified Goals: Investors often have diverse goals, from short-term income generation to long-term wealth preservation. By diversifying, you can tailor your portfolio to achieve your specific financial objectives.

4. Beyond Bitcoin: Where to Look:

Established Altcoins: Explore well-established cryptocurrencies like Ethereum, Litecoin, or Ripple, each with unique functionalities and a strong track record.

Utility-Based Projects: Invest in projects aiming to solve real-world problems in various sectors, offering potential utility and value beyond speculation.

Stablecoins: Consider incorporating stablecoins, pegged to real-world assets like fiat currencies, to provide stability and mitigate volatility within your portfolio.

Remember:

Research is Key: Don't blindly invest in any asset. Thoroughly research each project, understand its technology, and assess its long-term potential before investing.

Seek Professional Guidance: Consider consulting a financial advisor who can help you create a diversified portfolio aligned with your risk tolerance and financial goals.

By venturing beyond the allure of Bitcoin and embracing diversification, you can build a more resilient and potentially rewarding investment strategy, navigating the dynamic world of cryptocurrencies with greater confidence and control.

5 Chapter 5: Technical Analysis and Indicators

5.1 Technical Analysis

An introduction to key technical analysis tools and indicators that can assist investors in making informed decisions.

In the fast-paced world of cryptocurrency, making informed investment decisions requires more than just intuition or hype. Technical analysis (TA) provides valuable tools and indicators to analyze past price movements and identify potential future trends, empowering you to navigate the market with greater confidence. Let's explore some key TA tools to get you started.

1. Trend Analysis:

Trendlines: Identify the underlying direction of the market by connecting major swing highs and lows, helping you distinguish uptrends, downtrends, and consolidation periods.

Moving Averages: Calculate the average price over a specific period, smoothing out price fluctuations and revealing the overall trend direction. Common options include 50-day, 100-day, and 200-day moving averages.

2. Momentum Indicators:

Relative Strength Index (RSI): Measures the speed and magnitude of recent price movements, indicating potential overbought or oversold conditions. Readings above 70 suggest overbought territory, while values below 30 suggest oversold conditions.

Stochastic Oscillator: Similar to RSI, but compares the closing price to the price range within a specific period, identifying potential trend reversals.

3. Volume Analysis:

Trading Volume: Analyze the amount of cryptocurrency traded within a specific timeframe. Rising volume alongside rising prices often indicates strong buying pressure, while falling volume alongside rising prices might signal weakening momentum.

On-Balance Volume (OBV): Tracks the volume flow into and out of the market, providing insights into investor sentiment and potential buying/selling pressure.

4. Support and Resistance Levels:

Support: Price levels where buying pressure historically outweighs selling pressure, potentially halting or reversing downtrends.

Resistance: Price levels where selling pressure historically outweighs buying pressure, potentially halting or reversing uptrends.

Identifying these levels through historical price charts and volume analysis can inform entry and exit points for your trades.

Remember:

TA is not a crystal ball: TA indicators provide insights, not guarantees. Combine them with fundamental analysis and sound risk management practices.

Don't overcomplicate: Start with a few basic tools and master them before adding more complex indicators.

Develop your own strategy: Backtest your strategies on historical data and adjust them based on your risk tolerance and trading goals.

Further Exploration:

Explore additional TA indicators like Bollinger Bands, MACD, and Fibonacci retracements.

Familiarize yourself with charting patterns like head and shoulders or double bottoms for potential trend reversals.

Practice using TA tools on paper or demo accounts before risking real capital.

By understanding and incorporating these key TA tools, you can equip yourself to make informed decisions in the dynamic and ever-evolving world of cryptocurrency investing. Remember, responsible investment practices and continuous learning are crucial for navigating the market successfully.

Identifying common chart patterns and their implications for post-halving trading strategies.

As the Bitcoin halving draws near, investors worldwide scrutinize charts, searching for patterns that might hint at future price movements. While predicting the future remains impossible, understanding common chart patterns and their potential implications can equip you to formulate informed trading strategies in the post-halving landscape.

1. Ascending Triangle:

Shape: The price forms an upward trendline and a horizontal resistance line, creating a triangular pattern.

Implication: If the price breaks above the resistance line with increasing volume, it suggests a potential breakout and continuation of the uptrend. This could be bullish for post-halving trades.

Example: Look for historical instances of ascending triangles followed by breakouts after previous halving events.

2. Descending Triangle:

Shape: The price forms a downward trendline and a horizontal support line, creating a triangular pattern.

Implication: If the price breaks below the support line with increasing volume, it suggests a potential breakdown and continuation of the downtrend. This could be bearish for post-halving trades.

Caution: Descending triangles often precede significant price drops. Consider risk management strategies like stop-loss orders.

3. Head and Shoulders:

Shape: The price forms a high point (head), followed by two lower highs (shoulders) and a neckline connecting the lows.

Implication: A break below the neckline confirms a trend reversal from bullish to bearish. While historically seen after halvings, interpret cautiously due to potential false breakouts.

Example: Analyze past instances of head and shoulders patterns formed before and after halving events to assess their effectiveness.

4. Double Bottom:

Shape: The price forms two consecutive lows at roughly the same level, followed by an upward move and a neckline connecting the highs.

Implication: A break above the neckline confirms a trend reversal from bearish to bullish. This could be a signal for potential buying opportunities after the halving.

Remember: Double bottoms don't guarantee immediate upward trends. Monitor for confirmation and volume to support the breakout.

5. Cup and Handle:

Shape: The price forms a rounded bottom (cup) followed by a smaller pullback (handle).

Implication: A break above the handle's high suggests a continuation of the uptrend that formed the cup. This could be bullish for post-halving trades.

Consider: The depth and symmetry of the cup and handle influence the pattern's reliability. Analyze historical examples for better understanding.

Remember:

Chart patterns are not guarantees: Use them in conjunction with technical indicators, fundamental analysis, and risk management strategies.

Context matters: Interpret patterns within the broader market context, considering external factors and overall sentiment.

Backtest and adapt: Test these patterns on historical data to understand their effectiveness and adapt your strategies based on your findings.

By familiarizing yourself with these common chart patterns and their potential implications, you can gain valuable insights and formulate more informed trading strategies as you navigate the dynamic post-halving landscape. Remember, responsible trading practices, continuous learning, and a healthy dose of caution are crucial for navigating the ever-evolving world of cryptocurrency.

Incorporating fundamental analysis to evaluate the long-term prospects of Bitcoin.

While technical analysis provides valuable insights into short-term price movements, understanding Bitcoin's long-term potential requires delving deeper into its fundamental characteristics. Fundamental analysis (FA) examines the underlying factors that influence the value of an asset, offering a broader perspective to inform your investment decisions. Let's explore some key aspects of Bitcoin's fundamentals.

1. Scarcity and Supply Dynamics:

Finite Supply: Unlike fiat currencies with an ever-increasing supply, Bitcoin has a fixed limit of 21 million coins, creating scarcity and potentially contributing to long-term value appreciation.

Halving Events: Every four years, the block reward for mining new Bitcoins is halved, further reducing the rate of new coin creation and potentially impacting supply and demand dynamics.

Adoption and Network Effects: The increasing adoption of Bitcoin as a store of value, medium of exchange, or for other purposes can contribute to its long-term value as its network effect strengthens.

2. Technology and Security:

Blockchain Technology: The underlying blockchain technology powering Bitcoin offers inherent security, transparency, and immutability, potentially attracting users and developers building applications on top of it.

Scalability and Transaction Fees: Addressing scalability issues and reducing transaction fees are crucial for wider adoption and long-term usability. Analyze ongoing development efforts and potential solutions.

Security Risks: Cryptocurrencies are vulnerable to hacks and exploits. Evaluate Bitcoin's security measures and the community's efforts to mitigate risks.

3. Regulatory Landscape:

Government Regulations: Evolving regulations surrounding cryptocurrencies can significantly impact their adoption and value. Stay informed about regulatory developments and their potential implications.

Institutional Adoption: Growing involvement of institutional investors like banks and asset managers can legitimize Bitcoin and contribute to its long-term stability.

Central Bank Digital Currencies (CBDCs): The potential launch of CBDCs by central banks could pose competition or offer opportunities for collaboration. Analyze potential scenarios and their impact on Bitcoin.

4. Alternative Cryptocurrencies:

Competitive Landscape: Bitcoin faces competition from other cryptocurrencies offering different functionalities or features. Analyze their potential impact on Bitcoin's long-term dominance.

Innovation and Emerging Use Cases: Consider the potential for new use cases and technological advancements within the broader cryptocurrency ecosystem and their implications for Bitcoin's relevance.

Remember:

FA is not a crystal ball: It provides insights but not guarantees. Combine it with technical analysis and sound risk management practices.

Focus on long-term potential: FA helps assess Bitcoin's potential over extended periods, not short-term price movements.

Continuous research is key: The cryptocurrency landscape is dynamic. Stay updated on developments and adapt your analysis accordingly.

By incorporating fundamental analysis, you can gain a deeper understanding of the factors driving Bitcoin's long-term prospects, enabling you to make informed investment decisions aligned with your own risk tolerance and financial goals.

6 Chapter 6: Navigating Regulatory Challenges

6.1 Regulatory Landscape

Understanding the potential impact of regulatory developments on the cryptocurrency market.

The world of cryptocurrencies, characterized by innovation and disruption, often finds itself in the crosshairs of regulations. While regulatory uncertainties have been a constant companion for this young industry, recent developments suggest a turning point. Let's explore the potential impact of these changes on the cryptocurrency market:

1. The Regulatory Landscape:

Global Initiatives: Regulatory bodies worldwide are collaborating to establish frameworks for overseeing cryptocurrencies. This could bring much-needed clarity and stability to the market.

Varying Approaches: Different countries are taking diverse approaches, ranging from restrictive bans to innovation-friendly sandboxes. This creates complex scenarios for global players.

Focus Areas: Anti-money laundering (AML), know-your-customer (KYC) compliance, and consumer protection are key areas of regulatory focus. This could improve transparency and trust.

2. Potential Impacts:

Short-Term Volatility: Regulatory announcements often trigger market fluctuations, presenting both opportunities and risks for investors.

Increased Scrutiny: Exchanges and projects face stricter compliance requirements, potentially leading to consolidation and higher barriers to entry.

Mainstream Adoption: Clear regulations could pave the way for institutional investors and traditional finance to enter the market, boosting liquidity and stability.

Innovation: Stringent regulations might stifle innovation, while flexible frameworks could foster responsible development of new projects and use cases.

3. Navigating the Future:

Stay Informed: Keep track of regulatory developments in key jurisdictions and their potential impact on specific projects and the overall market.

Diversify: Spread your investments across different cryptocurrencies and asset classes to mitigate risk associated with regulatory changes targeting specific projects or coins.

Understand the Project: Choose projects with strong fundamentals, clear roadmaps, and a commitment to regulatory compliance.

Seek Professional Guidance: Consult a financial advisor with expertise in cryptocurrencies to navigate the complex regulatory landscape and make informed investment decisions.

Remember:

The regulatory landscape is evolving rapidly, making it difficult to predict the full impact.

Regulations aim to protect consumers and ensure financial stability, not necessarily hinder innovation.

Responsible investors stay informed, adapt to changes, and focus on long-term value propositions of projects they support.

By understanding the potential impact of regulatory developments and adopting a proactive approach, you can navigate the dynamic cryptocurrency market with greater confidence and make informed decisions aligned with your risk tolerance and investment goals.

Highlighting the importance of complying with regulations and securing digital assets.

The explosive growth of the cryptocurrency market has brought immense excitement and opportunity, but also inherent risks. As individuals and businesses increasingly delve into this dynamic realm, compliance with regulations and securing digital assets become paramount for navigating the landscape safely and responsibly.

1. Compliance: Building Trust and Stability:

Regulatory landscape: Governments worldwide are grappling with regulating cryptocurrencies, aiming to prevent illegal activities and protect consumers. Adherence to evolving regulations fosters trust, attracts responsible players, and promotes long-term market stability.

Understanding KYC/AML: Know-Your-Customer (KYC) and Anti-Money Laundering (AML) regulations help combat financial crime and protect users. Staying compliant demonstrates responsible participation in the ecosystem.

Tax implications: Depending on your jurisdiction, cryptocurrency holdings and transactions may have tax implications. Understanding and complying with tax laws ensures transparency and avoids legal repercussions.

2. Security: Protecting Your Precious Assets:

Secure storage: Implement robust security measures like strong passwords, two-factor authentication, and hardware wallets to safeguard your digital assets from unauthorized access.

Beware of scams: Phishing attacks, social engineering, and malware specifically target crypto users. Exercise caution, verify information, and never share sensitive details with unsolicited contacts.

Choose reputable platforms: Utilize established and regulated crypto exchanges and platforms with proven security track records to minimize risk of hacks and fraud.

Stay informed: Keep yourself updated on emerging security threats and best practices. Educate yourself and others on responsible handling of digital assets.

3. Why it Matters:

Peace of mind: Complying with regulations and securing your assets reduces stress and ensures you participate in the crypto market with confidence.

Avoiding legal trouble: Non-compliance with regulations can lead to hefty fines, legal action, and reputational damage. Secure practices minimize the risk of theft and loss.

Building a sustainable future: A secure and compliant crypto ecosystem attracts greater adoption, fosters innovation, and ultimately benefits all participants.

Remember:

Compliance and security are ongoing processes, not one-time actions. Stay vigilant and adapt your practices as regulations evolve and security threats emerge.

Seek professional guidance when needed. Crypto regulations can be complex, and security solutions vary. Consult with experts to tailor your approach based on your unique needs and risk tolerance.

By prioritizing compliance and security, you become a responsible steward of your digital assets, contribute to a healthier crypto ecosystem, and pave the way for a more secure and prosperous future in this exciting new frontier.

Examining the role of institutional investors and their influence on the market post-halving.

As the Bitcoin halving event approaches, speculation intensifies about its potential impact on the cryptocurrency market. One crucial factor worth examining is the growing role of institutional investors. Their involvement has the potential to significantly influence the market dynamics post-halving, bringing both opportunities and challenges for various stakeholders.

1. The Rise of Institutional Interest:

Maturing Market: As the cryptocurrency market matures, it attracts an increasing number of institutional investors like hedge funds, asset managers, and pension funds. This is driven by:

Potential for high returns: Bitcoin's historical performance and inherent scarcity entice investors seeking diversification and alpha generation.

Evolving infrastructure: Improved custody solutions, regulated exchanges, and clearer regulations contribute to a more institutional-friendly environment.

Shifting perspectives: Growing acceptance of cryptocurrencies as an asset class and potential inflation hedges further fuels institutional interest.

2. Potential Impacts of Institutional Involvement:

Increased Liquidity: Large-scale inflows from institutions can increase market liquidity, potentially reducing volatility and making price discovery more efficient.

Price Appreciation: Increased demand from institutions could drive up prices, benefiting existing investors and attracting new participants.

Mainstream Adoption: Institutional involvement can legitimize the market, attracting traditional investors and accelerating broader adoption of cryptocurrencies.

Regulatory Scrutiny: Increased institutional participation might invite greater regulatory scrutiny, potentially impacting market dynamics and project development.

3. Challenges and Considerations:

Infrastructure Gaps: Existing infrastructure might not fully accommodate the needs of large institutions, requiring ongoing development and scaling.

Regulatory Uncertainty: Evolving regulatory landscapes pose challenges for institutions seeking clear guidelines and long-term stability.

Volatility Concerns: Institutions might be hesitant to enter due to the inherent volatility of the cryptocurrency market.

4. Navigating the Future:

Understanding the Landscape: Investors and projects should stay informed about institutional trends, preferences, and regulatory developments.

Tailoring Strategies: Projects can adapt their offerings and communication to appeal to institutional investors seeking specific functionalities and compliance standards.

Risk Management: Investors should carefully assess risks associated with volatility, regulations, and project-specific factors before making investment decisions.

Conclusion:

The increasing involvement of institutional investors in the cryptocurrency market represents a significant turning point. While it presents exciting opportunities for growth and mainstream adoption, it also necessitates careful consideration of potential challenges and regulatory landscapes. By understanding the dynamics at play and adopting strategic approaches, various stakeholders can navigate the post-halving landscape with greater clarity and preparedness, shaping a more robust and inclusive future for the crypto ecosystem.

7.1   Industry Trends:

Exploring the broader trends and developments in the cryptocurrency space.

While Bitcoin remains the dominant force in the cryptocurrency landscape, its influence extends far beyond just its own price movements. The broader crypto space is teeming with innovations, trends, and developments that are shaping the future of finance, technology, and even society as a whole. Let's explore some of the most exciting areas to watch:

1. Decentralized Finance (DeFi):

Empowering individuals: DeFi offers financial services like lending, borrowing, and trading directly between users, bypassing traditional intermediaries. This fosters financial inclusion and empowers individuals with greater control over their finances.

Evolving protocols: New DeFi protocols are constantly emerging, offering innovative features like automated market makers (AMMs) and flash loans, expanding the possibilities within the ecosystem.

Regulatory focus: As DeFi gains traction, regulators are closely scrutinizing its potential risks and exploring frameworks to ensure stability and consumer protection.

2. Non-Fungible Tokens (NFTs):

Digital ownership: NFTs represent unique digital assets like artwork, collectibles, or even virtual land, enabling digital ownership and facilitating new forms of creativity and monetization.

Beyond art: NFTs are expanding beyond collectibles, finding applications in gaming, supply chain management, and even identity verification.

Scalability challenges: High transaction fees and scalability issues on popular NFT platforms remain hurdles for wider adoption.

3. Central Bank Digital Currencies (CBDCs):

Digital fiat: Central banks worldwide are exploring the development of CBDCs, digital versions of their national currencies. This could potentially enhance efficiency, transparency, and financial inclusion.

Impact on crypto: CBDCs could compete with or complement existing cryptocurrencies, depending on their design and implementation.

Privacy concerns: Balancing individual privacy with central bank oversight remains a key challenge in CBDC development.

4. Metaverse and Web3:

Immersive experiences: The metaverse promises a future of interconnected virtual worlds powered by blockchain technology, potentially revolutionizing social interaction, gaming, and even work.

Web3 a decentralized future: Web3 aims to create a more decentralized and user-owned internet, leveraging blockchain technology and cryptocurrencies.

Early stages: These concepts are still in their early stages, but their potential impact on various industries is significant.

5. Sustainability and Green Crypto:

Energy consumption: Proof-of-work consensus mechanisms used by Bitcoin and other cryptocurrencies raise concerns about energy consumption.

Alternative options: Projects utilizing more energy-efficient consensus mechanisms like Proof-of-Stake are gaining traction to address sustainability concerns.

Growing awareness: As environmental consciousness increases, sustainable crypto solutions are becoming increasingly important for long-term viability.

Remember:

The cryptocurrency space is dynamic and constantly evolving. Stay informed about emerging trends and developments to navigate this exciting, complex landscape effectively.

Conduct your own research before investing in any cryptocurrency project. Understand the technology, the team behind it, and the potential risks involved.

Diversify your portfolio and manage your risk wisely. The crypto market is inherently volatile, so responsible investment practices are crucial.

By exploring these broader trends and staying informed, you can gain a deeper understanding of the potential impact of cryptocurrency on the future and make informed decisions as we navigate this ever-evolving technological and financial landscape.

Analyzing the potential role of Bitcoin in the future of finance and global economies.

Bitcoin, the first and most prominent cryptocurrency, has captured the imagination of many as a potential revolution in finance. While its future remains uncertain, understanding its potential role in shaping the future of finance and global economies is crucial for informed decision-making and navigating this transformative landscape.

1. Potential Benefits:

Financial Inclusion: Bitcoin's borderless and permissionless nature offers access to financial services for individuals excluded from traditional systems, promoting financial inclusion in developing economies.

Transparency and Immutability: The blockchain technology underlying Bitcoin provides transparency and immutability of transactions, potentially reducing fraud and increasing trust in financial systems.

Faster and Cheaper Transactions: Compared to traditional systems, Bitcoin transactions can be faster and cheaper, especially for cross-border payments, potentially benefiting businesses and individuals.

Store of Value: Some view Bitcoin as a potential "digital gold," a scarce and secure store of value in a world of fiat currency inflation.

2. Potential Challenges:

Volatility: Bitcoin's extreme price volatility makes it unsuitable for everyday transactions and poses challenges for mainstream adoption.

Scalability: The current Bitcoin network struggles to handle large transaction volumes, potentially limiting its scalability and global reach.

Energy Consumption: The energy-intensive proof-of-work consensus mechanism raises environmental concerns and sustainability questions.

Regulation: Evolving regulations and uncertainties surrounding the legal status of cryptocurrencies create challenges for wider adoption and integration with traditional financial systems.

3. Potential Impact on Global Economies:

Reserve Currencies: Some argue that Bitcoin could challenge the dominance of traditional reserve currencies like the US dollar, although its volatility and regulatory hurdles remain significant obstacles.

International Trade: Bitcoin could potentially facilitate faster and cheaper cross-border transactions, impacting international trade and financial flows.

Central Bank Control: The decentralized nature of Bitcoin could challenge central banks' control over monetary policy, raising complex economic and governance questions.

4. Future Scenarios:

Mainstream Adoption: If regulatory hurdles are addressed and scalability issues are solved, Bitcoin could see wider adoption as a payment method or store of value.

Niche Use Case: Bitcoin might remain a niche asset for specific use cases like international payments or digital gold.

Regulation and Integration: Regulatory frameworks and collaboration with traditional finance could lead to integration of Bitcoin and other cryptocurrencies into the existing financial system.

Remember:

This is not financial advice. Conduct your own research and understand the risks involved before investing in any cryptocurrency.

Stay informed about the evolving landscape of Bitcoin, regulations, and broader economic trends to make informed decisions.

The future of finance is likely to be multifaceted, with Bitcoin potentially playing a role alongside traditional systems and emerging innovations.

Cultivating a resilient and patient mindset for long-term success in the cryptocurrency market.

The cryptocurrency market, often described as a rollercoaster ride, demands a unique approach. While the lure of quick gains is seductive, long-term success hinges on cultivating a resilient and patient mindset. Let's explore how to navigate this dynamic landscape with composure and strategic thinking:

1. Building Resilience:

Emotional Intelligence: Recognize and manage emotions like fear and greed that can cloud judgment. Practice mindfulness and breathing techniques to stay calm during market swings.

Focus on Fundamentals: Don't be swayed by hype or FOMO (fear of missing out). Analyze projects based on their underlying technology, team, and long-term potential, not short-term price movements.

Expect Volatility: Understand that volatility is inherent to the market. Don't panic sell during dips; view them as potential buying opportunities if aligned with your strategy.

Diversify Wisely: Spread your investments across different cryptocurrencies and asset classes to mitigate risk and avoid overexposure to any single project.

Build a Support Network: Connect with other responsible investors and communities to share insights, learn from each other, and maintain healthy perspectives.

2. Embracing Patience:

Long-Term Horizon: Invest with a view of years, not days or weeks. Focus on projects with strong potential for long-term growth and value creation.

Ignore Daily Noise: Avoid obsessing over daily price movements. Focus on your investment thesis and stay patient even during periods of slow growth.

Time in the Market: Remember, successful investors often emphasize "time in the market" over "timing the market." Consistent participation, not market predictions, holds the key.

Set Realistic Expectations: Don't expect overnight riches. Understand that even promising projects require time to develop and mature.

Reward Progress, Not Perfection: Celebrate milestones and incremental gains as markers of progress on your long-term investment journey.

Remember:

No Guarantees: The cryptocurrency market is inherently unpredictable. While resilience and patience increase your chances of success, there are no guarantees.

Continuous Learning: Stay informed about market trends, technological advancements, and regulatory developments to adapt your strategy as needed.

Don't Invest What You Can't Afford: Invest only what you can afford to lose and avoid risking money crucial for your essential needs.

Seek Professional Guidance: Consider consulting a financial advisor with expertise in cryptocurrencies, especially if you are a beginner or have complex needs.

By cultivating a resilient and patient mindset, you can equip yourself to navigate the ups and downs of the cryptocurrency market with greater confidence and composure. Remember, this is a marathon, not a sprint. By focusing on fundamentals, managing emotions, and embracing a long-term perspective, you can increase your chances of achieving success in this exciting and ever-evolving landscape.

8 Conclusion:

While Bitcoin's future role in shaping finance and global economies remains uncertain, it presents both opportunities and challenges.

Analyzing its potential impact requires careful consideration of its benefits, limitations, and evolving landscape.

As the technology matures and regulations develop, Bitcoin's influence will likely be felt in some form, requiring individuals and institutions to adapt and navigate this dynamic and transformative era.

"Bitcoin Halving 2024: A Guide for Investors" aims to empower readers with the knowledge and tools necessary to navigate the post-halving landscape effectively.

By understanding the dynamics of the halving event and implementing informed investment strategies, readers can position themselves to make the most of the opportunities presented by the evolving cryptocurrency market.

Remember, investing in Bitcoin carries inherent risks, and it is crucial to conduct thorough research and seek professional advice before making any investment decisions.

The End

By Mohamed Elwardany